Looking at X-rays

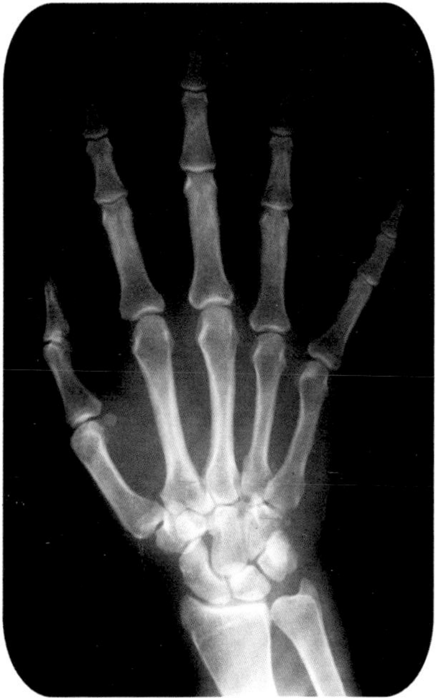

by Kris Bonnell

Look at the hand.

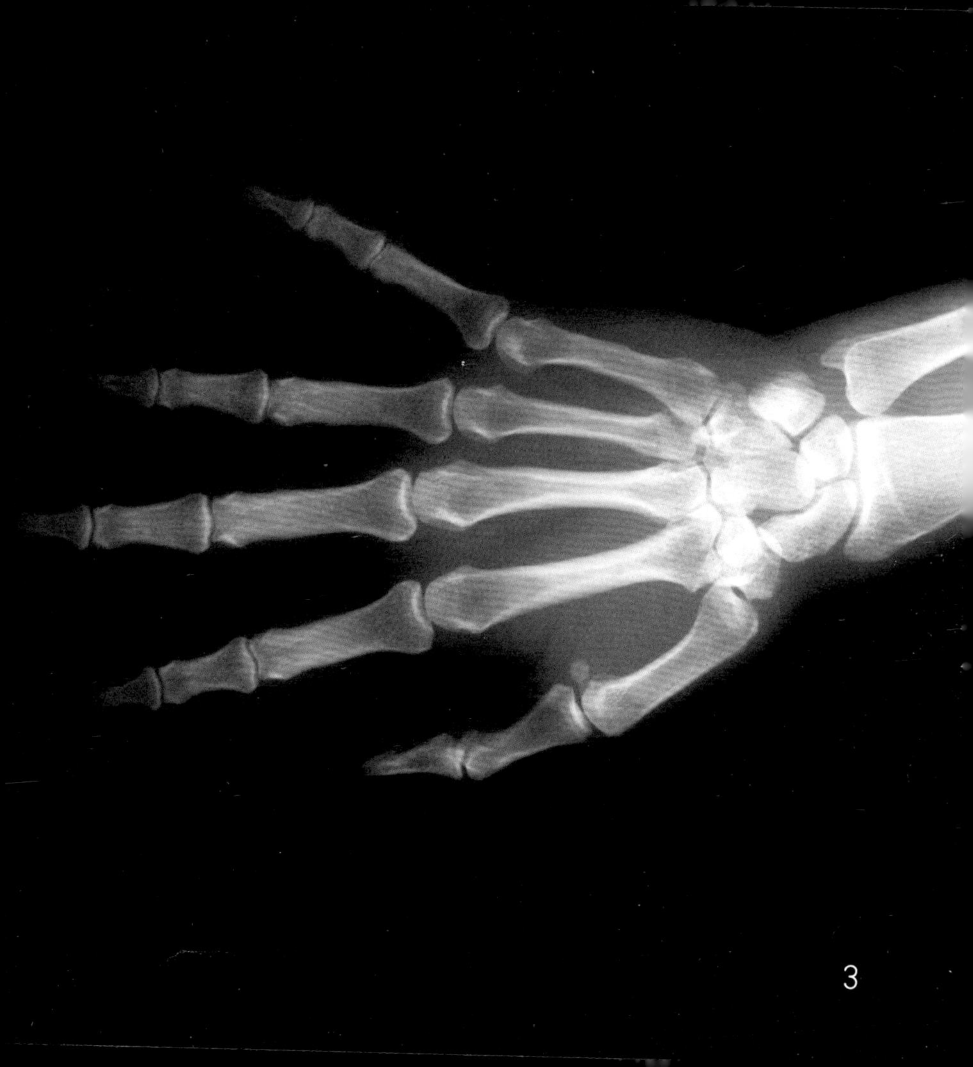

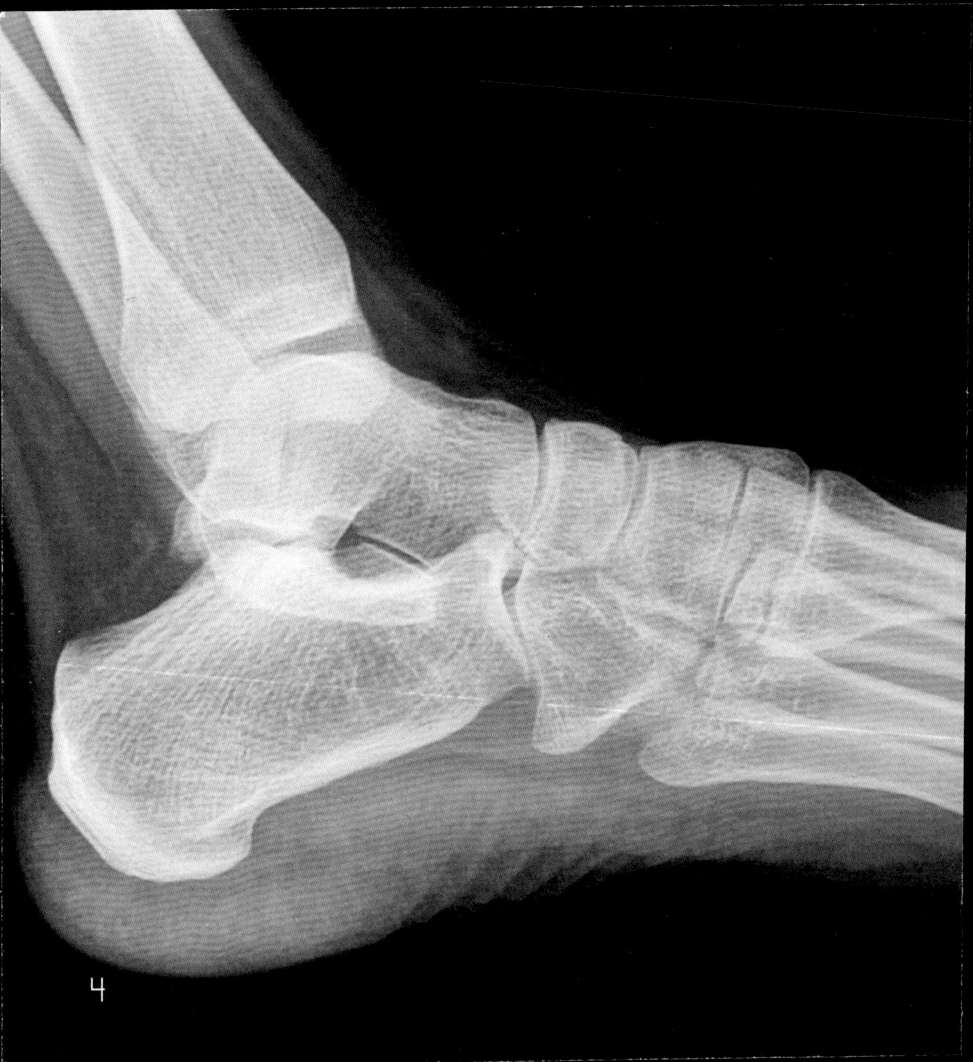

4

Look at the foot.

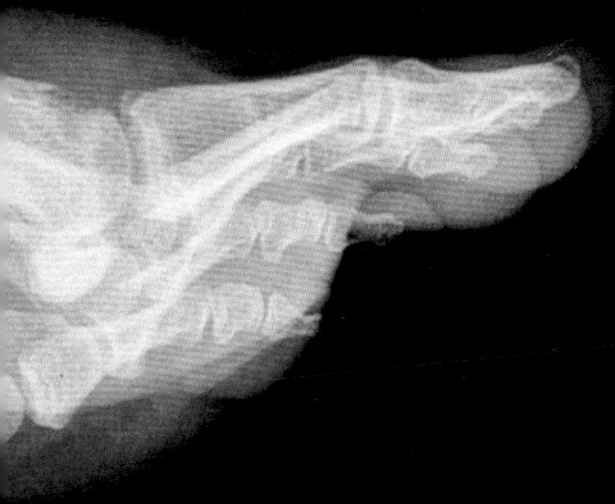

Look at the teeth.

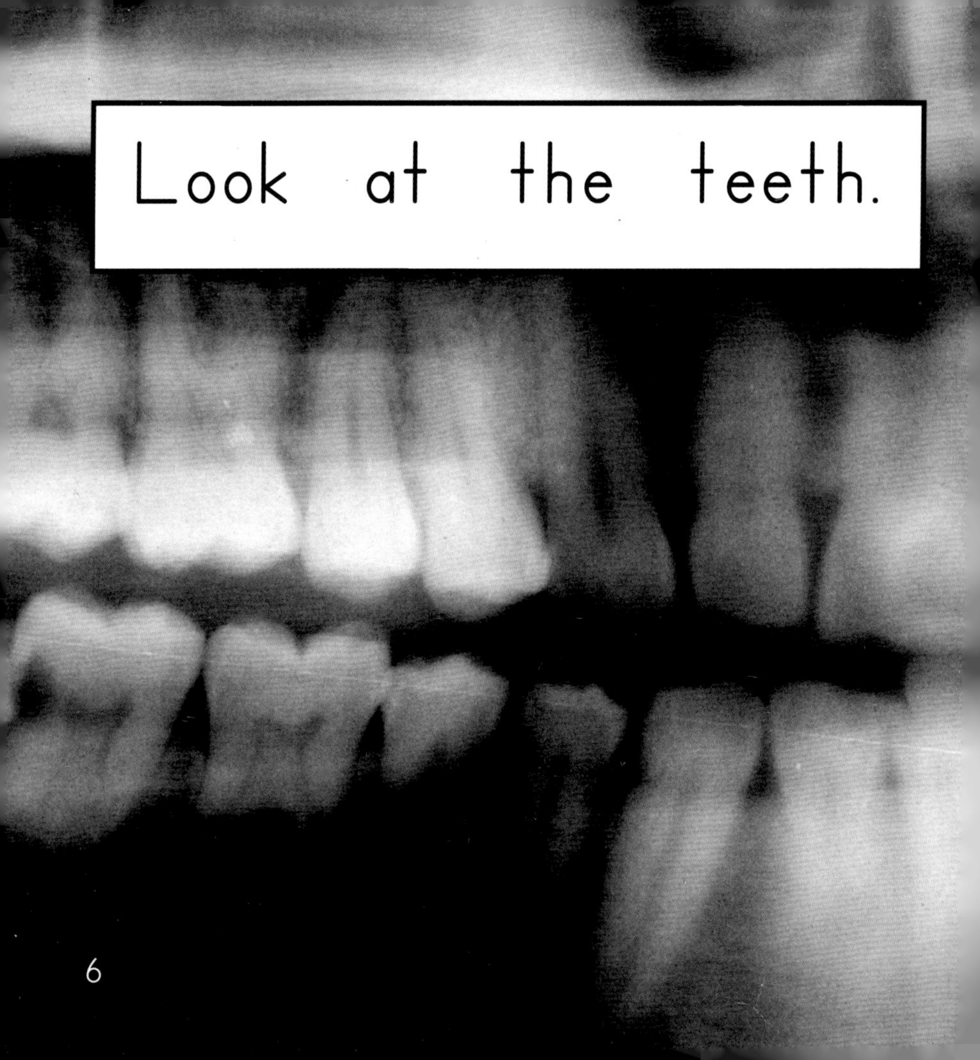

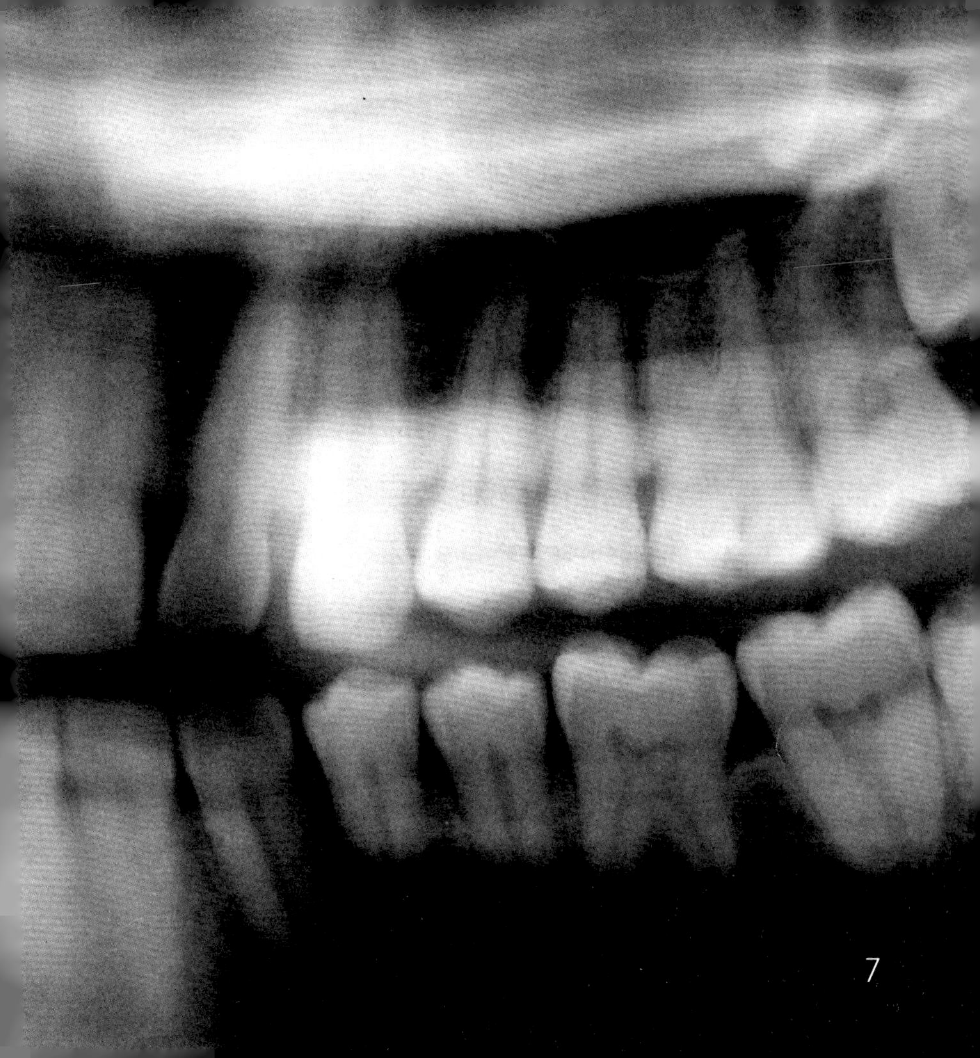

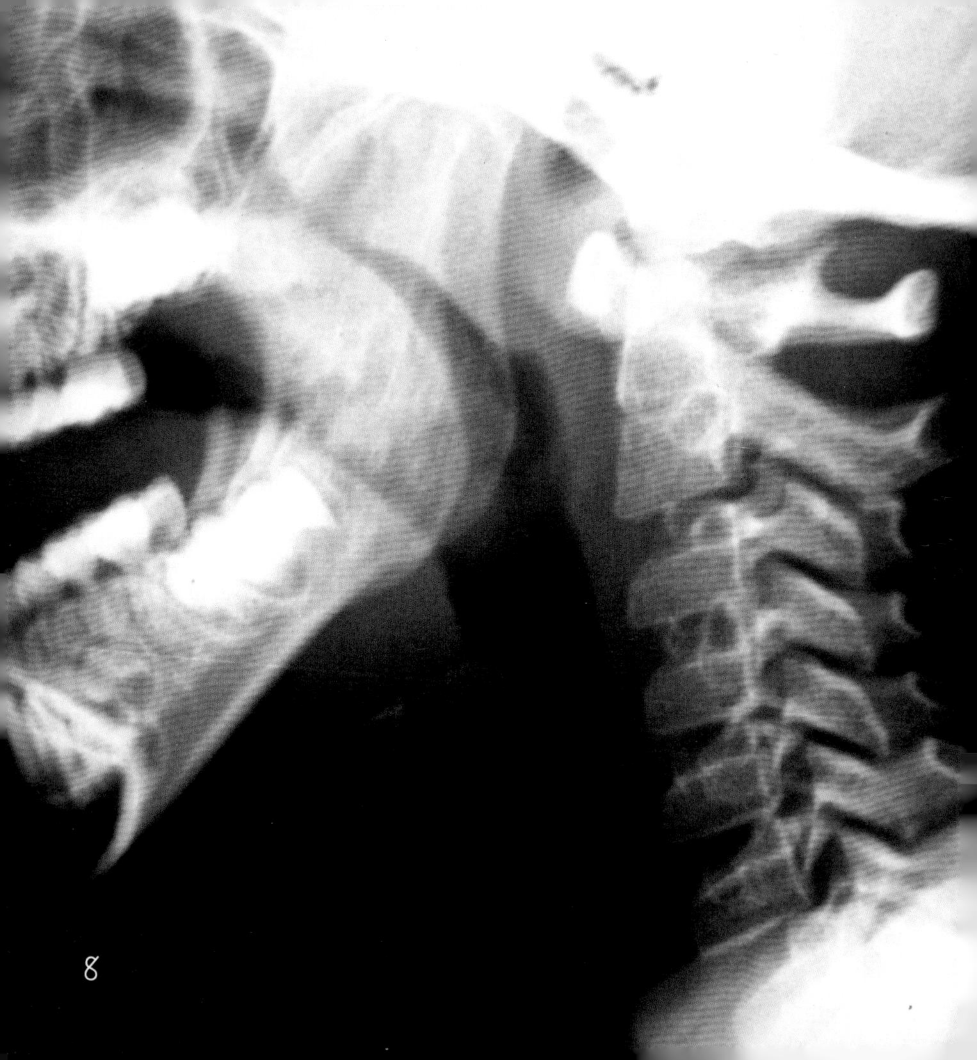

Look at the neck.

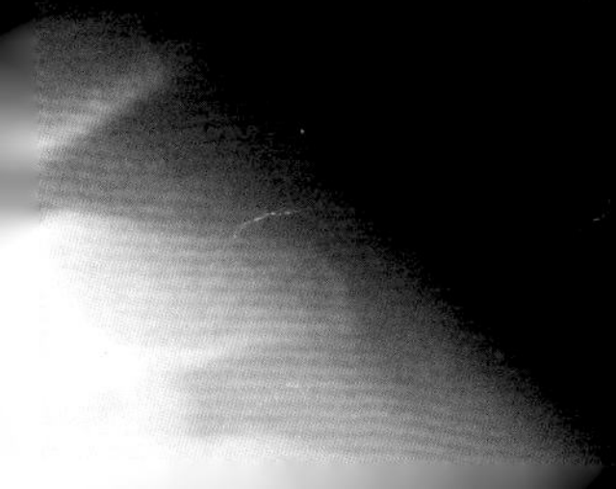

Look at the head.

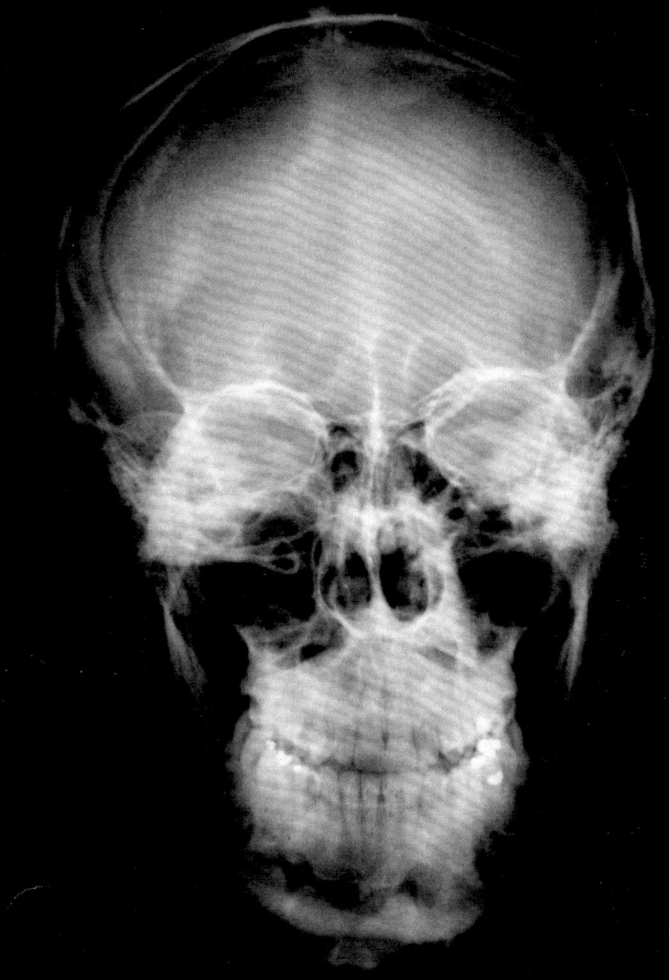

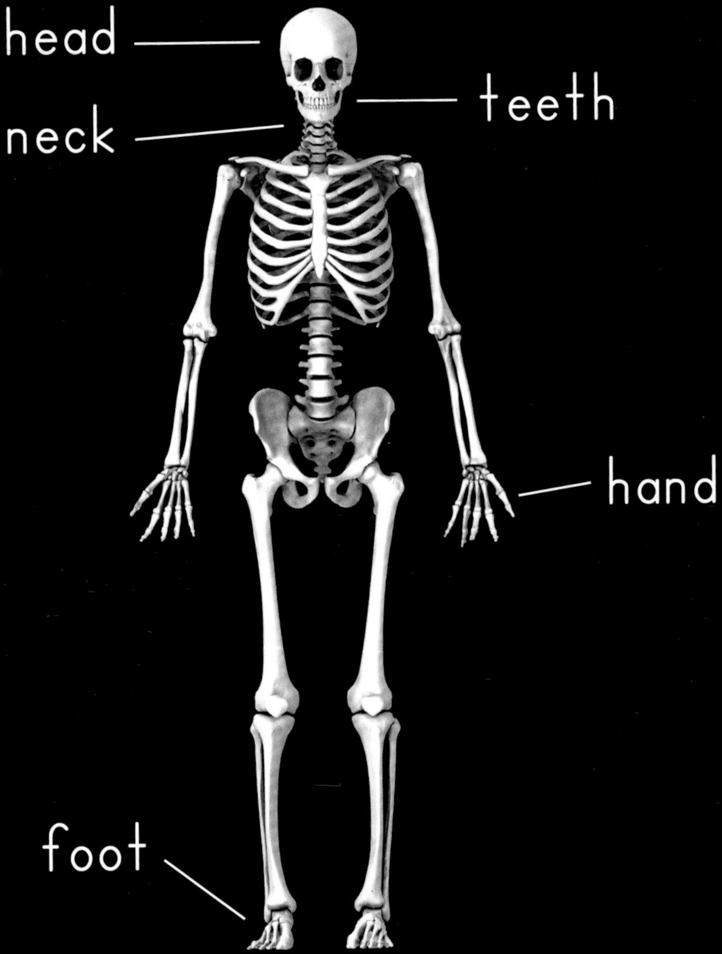
head
teeth
neck
hand
foot